BIGGEST NAMES IN SPORTS

ANTONIO BROWN

FOOTBALL STAR

by Alex Monnig

D1532584

FOCUS
READERS

WWW.FOCUSREADERS.COM

Focus Readers is distributed by North Star Editions:
sales@northstareditions.com | 888-417-0195

Produced for Focus Readers by Red Line Editorial.

Photographs ©: Evan Pinkus/AP Images, cover, 1; Perry Knotts/AP Images, 4–5, 7; Scott Boehm/AP Images, 8–9; Al Goldis/AP Images, 10; Andy Jacobsohn/Icon Sportswire, 13; Michael Conroy/AP Images, 15; Robert Smith/The Leaf-Chronicle/AP Images, 16–17; Matt Slocum/AP Images, 19; Don Wright/AP Images, 21, 22–23, 24; Larry Roberts/Pittsburgh Post-Gazette/AP Images, 27; Red Line Editorial, 29

ISBN
978-1-63517-484-7 (hardcover)
978-1-63517-556-1 (paperback)
978-1-63517-700-8 (ebook pdf)
978-1-63517-628-5 (hosted ebook)

Library of Congress Control Number: 2017948066

Printed in the United States of America
Mankato, MN
November, 2017

ABOUT THE AUTHOR

Alex Monnig is a freelance journalist from St. Louis, Missouri, who now lives in Sydney, Australia. He graduated with a master's degree from the University of Missouri in 2010. During his career, he has spent time covering sporting events around the world and has written more than 20 children's books.

TABLE OF CONTENTS

CHAPTER 1

PLAYOFF MAGIC

Antonio Brown was ready to play. He and the Pittsburgh Steelers were hosting the Miami Dolphins in the **playoffs**. Brown knew that the 2016 season would be over for the losing team. And he was going to make sure his Steelers came out on top.

Brown pumps up the crowd during his introduction.

Early in the first quarter, Pittsburgh had the ball at the 50-yard line. Steelers quarterback Ben Roethlisberger took the snap. Then he threw a quick pass to Brown near the **line of scrimmage**.

Brown took care of the rest. He sprinted past a group of six defenders and bolted down the **sideline**. One more defender tried to dive at Brown's feet, but it was too late. Brown was gone. He ran into the end zone and celebrated the game's first touchdown.

The crowd went wild. But Brown knew his job wasn't done yet. A few minutes later, the Steelers had the ball at their own 38-yard line. Roethlisberger fired a

Brown runs past Dolphins defenders as he finds his way to the end zone.

pass over the middle. Brown caught the ball near midfield, and he was off to the races. Fans rose to their feet as Brown scored his second touchdown of the quarter.

The Steelers went on to win the game 30–12. And Brown had played a huge role in the team's victory.

CHAPTER 2

FIGHTING TO MAKE IT

Antonio Brown has made millions of dollars playing in the National Football League (NFL). But he started his life just trying to survive the rough streets of Miami, Florida. Antonio was born on July 10, 1988. He lived in a part of Miami known as Liberty City.

Brown runs for extra yards against the Purdue Boilermakers in a 2007 game.

Brown makes an amazing grab during a two-point conversion attempt.

The area was full of poverty, violence, and drug use.

Antonio's family situation was a tough one. He did not know his father very well. And Antonio did not get along with his stepfather. So Antonio stopped living with his mother and stepfather when he was just 16 years old. Antonio had to live with friends and coaches. Sometimes his friends would get robbed. Other times they would get arrested for committing crimes themselves.

Antonio used football as an escape from his troubles. It was one of the only things he had fun doing. At Miami Norland High School, he starred at multiple positions. However, he struggled in class.

Antonio wanted to go to Florida State University. Unfortunately, his grades were not strong enough to get into the school.

So he spent one year at North Carolina Tech to improve his grades.

Brown played quarterback during the 2006 season at North Carolina Tech. He was good enough to earn a **scholarship** to Florida International University. But then he had more off-field trouble. Brown was involved in an argument one night

RUNS IN THE FAMILY

Antonio Brown is not the only player from his family to make a name on the football field. His father, "Touchdown" Eddie Brown, was the most valuable player (MVP) of the Arena Football League twice. In addition, Antonio's younger brother, Desmond, played at the University of Pittsburgh.

Brown played a big role in the Central Michigan offense.

before the season started. Coaches

kicked him off the team.

   Still, Brown got one more opportunity.

He was invited to try out as a walk-on

at Central Michigan University (CMU).

Within a week of practice, his athleticism and skill had earned him a scholarship.

Brown was a star in his three years at CMU. By the time he left, he was among the school's all-time leaders in **receptions**, receiving yards, and receiving touchdowns.

Even after recording huge numbers in college, NFL **scouts** didn't think much of Brown. Many coaches believed he was too small. They also didn't think he could run the complicated **routes** of NFL offenses.

Brown fell to the sixth round of the 2010 NFL **Draft**. The Pittsburgh Steelers finally selected him with the 195th pick overall. There were 21 wide receivers

Brown shows his speed for NFL scouts in 2010.

selected before him. But it wouldn't be long before Brown started making the teams that passed on him look foolish.

CHAPTER 3

MAKING A NAME IN THE NFL

Antonio Brown's NFL career started with a bang. The first time he touched the ball, he scored a touchdown on a kickoff return. However, the rest of his rookie season in 2010 was mostly quiet. He did not score any other touchdowns that year.

Brown runs back the opening kickoff against the Tennessee Titans.

The Steelers had a strong group of wide receivers led by Hines Ward and Mike Wallace. They were the main targets for Steelers quarterback Ben Roethlisberger. That meant Brown had to wait for a chance to make a name for himself.

He started doing exactly that in the playoffs after the 2010 season. The

KEEPING TRACK

In the 2010 NFL Draft, all 32 teams passed on Brown. That motivated Brown to do some math. $8 \times 4 = 32$. That's why Brown chose jersey No. 84. He said wearing the number would give him more motivation to prove to everybody that they were wrong.

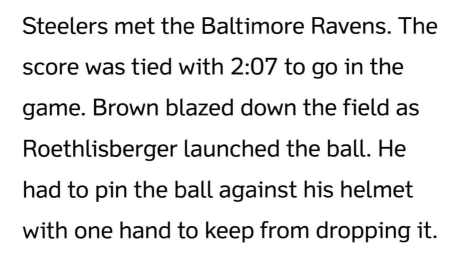

Brown makes an unbelievable catch in a playoff game against the Ravens.

Steelers met the Baltimore Ravens. The score was tied with 2:07 to go in the game. Brown blazed down the field as Roethlisberger launched the ball. He had to pin the ball against his helmet with one hand to keep from dropping it.

But somehow he caught it. Brown went out of bounds three yards from the end zone, putting the Steelers in position to score. The Steelers won the game 31–24.

The next season, Brown made plenty more big plays. He had always been great at catching tough passes. But the extra things he did made him even tougher to stop. He studied opponents to see how they would cover him. He also worked on planting his feet as soon as he caught the ball.

In 2011, Brown was targeted more than any other Steelers receiver. He racked up 1,108 receiving yards. He also had 1,062 yards on kick returns. That made

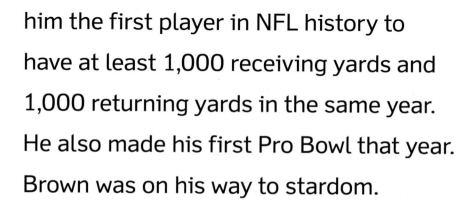

Brown made a name for himself with his blazing speed.

him the first player in NFL history to
have at least 1,000 receiving yards and
1,000 returning yards in the same year.
He also made his first Pro Bowl that year.
Brown was on his way to stardom.

CHAPTER 4

REACHING THE TOP

An ankle injury kept Brown on the sidelines for a few games during the 2012 season. But in 2013, he came back stronger than ever. By that time, Hines Ward and Mike Wallace were no longer on the team. Fortunately, Brown was ready to be Pittsburgh's top wide receiver.

Brown hauls in a touchdown during a 2016 game against the New York Giants.

Brown's ability to avoid defenders makes him a major threat.

He finished the year with 1,499 yards, eight touchdowns, and another Pro Bowl appearance.

Brown was even better in 2014. He led the league with 129 receptions and 1,698 receiving yards. One of his best plays came against the Indianapolis Colts. Brown sprinted toward the back corner of the end zone. The Colts cornerback ran with him stride for stride. Brown kept his head turned toward the quarterback. The pass sailed over both players' heads. Brown lunged for the ball.

OFF THE FIELD, ONTO THE DANCE FLOOR

Fans are used to seeing Brown's moves on the field. But in 2016, they also got to see what he could do on the dance floor. Brown was on *Dancing with the Stars*, a show in which celebrities are paired with professional dancers. Brown put on quite a show and finished in fourth place.

He stuck out his left hand, plucking the pass from midair. He pulled it in to his body for a one-handed touchdown.

Sometimes Brown's high-energy play gets him into trouble. He has been fined several times for **excessive** touchdown celebrations. But fans love his electric attitude and effort on the field.

Brown is just as popular off the field. He is involved in the community in a variety of ways. For instance, he leads the annual Antonio Brown and Friends Softball Game. Brown and other NFL players play a game in Pittsburgh, Pennsylvania, to raise money for charities.

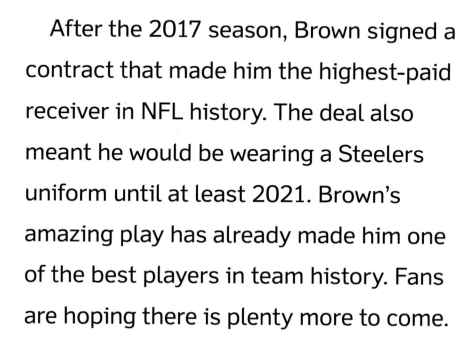

Brown runs a football camp for kids in the Pittsburgh area.

After the 2017 season, Brown signed a contract that made him the highest-paid receiver in NFL history. The deal also meant he would be wearing a Steelers uniform until at least 2021. Brown's amazing play has already made him one of the best players in team history. Fans are hoping there is plenty more to come.

ANTONIO BROWN

- Height: 5 feet 10 inches (178 cm)
- Weight: 180 pounds (82 kg)
- Birth date: July 10, 1988
- Birthplace: Miami, Florida
- High school: Miami Norland High School
- College: Central Michigan University, Mount Pleasant, Michigan (2007–2010)
- NFL team: Pittsburgh Steelers (2010–)
- Major awards: Pro Bowl (2011, 2013, 2014, 2015, 2016); First-Team All Pro (2014, 2015, 2016)

Pittsburgh

Mount Pleasant

Miami

FOCUS ON
ANTONIO BROWN

Write your answers on a separate piece of paper.

1. Write a paragraph about the obstacles Antonio Brown faced during his journey to the NFL.

2. What part of Antonio Brown's personality do you think helped him most in achieving his dream of playing in the NFL?

3. Where did Antonio Brown play college football?

    A. University of Miami
    B. Central Michigan University
    C. University of Pittsburgh

4. Why didn't Brown put up big numbers in 2010?

    A. because he didn't practice hard enough
    B. because the team already had two great receivers
    C. because the Steelers were not paying him enough

Answer key on page 32.

GLOSSARY

draft
A system that allows teams to acquire new players coming into a league.

excessive
More than necessary.

line of scrimmage
The yard-line on which a football play begins.

playoffs
A set of games played after the regular season to decide which team will be the champion.

receptions
Catches of forward passes.

routes
Directions that receivers run as they try to get open.

scholarship
Money given to a student to pay for education expenses.

scouts
People whose jobs involve looking for talented young players.

sideline
The boundary lines on the side of a football field.

TO LEARN MORE

BOOKS

Glave, Tom. *Pittsburgh Steelers*. Mankato, MN: The Child's World, 2015.

Graves, Will. *Pittsburgh Steelers*. Minneapolis: Abdo Publishing, 2017.

Morey, Allan. *The Pittsburgh Steelers Story*. Minneapolis: Bellwether Media, 2017.

NOTE TO EDUCATORS

Visit **www.focusreaders.com** to find lesson plans, activities, links, and other resources related to this title.

INDEX

Answer Key: **1.** Answers will vary; **2.** Answers will vary; **3.** B; **4.** B